What do you say t

What do you say to a MOONIE?

Chris Elkins

Tyndale House Publishers, Inc.   Wheaton, Illinois

Library of Congress Catalog Card Number 81-50848
ISBN 0-8423-7867-7
Copyright © 1981 by Chris Elkins.
All rights reserved.
First printing, July 1981.
Printed in the United States of America.

CONTENTS

1 I was a Moonie *7*

2 What are the Moonies like? *13*

3 What do the Moonies believe? *33*

4 What else should I know about the Moonies? *49*

5 Why do I feel defensive toward the Moonies? *63*

6 What do you say to a Moonie? *69*

7 For parents of Moonies *83*

ONE

I was a Moonie

For two and a half years I lived and worked, ate and slept, laughed and cried as a member of a cult. I was a Moonie.

It was a Moonie group on my college campus—a dozen or so bright young people with warm, friendly faces—which led me into a full-time commitment to the Unification Church. In a matter of weeks I dropped out of school, resigned as president of my fraternity, and quit my job at the bank. By the summer of 1973, I was selling flowers in parking lots for the Rev. Sun Myung Moon.

Back then, the Unification Church suffered from a severe case of anonymity. Few people had heard of the Moonies. It became the strategy of the Church to grab publicity, even notoriety, wherever it could be found. Soon posters bearing the face of the Rev. Moon were plastered on telephone poles along the streets of New York, Chicago, and San Francisco.

Moonies got into the headlines and were interviewed on TV. The Unification Church became active among government officials in Washington, D. C., and worked for the support of President Nixon during Watergate.

During this time I played a role in the "making of the Moonies." I was appointed to be the managing editor of a Moonie newspaper that operated discreetly on Capitol Hill. I attended White House parties and worked closely with the Unification Church president, Neil Salonen. And on several occasions, my work carried me into the very presence of the Rev. Sun Myung Moon himself.

On the home front, my parents, whose love for me never faltered, sought help from a deprogrammer. A "kidnapping" was set up for Christmas 1975. Home for my brother's wedding in December, I caught wind of the scheme. On Christmas Eve I made a tearful and harrowing escape.

Hindsight is often *insight* into the power of God. By this time I had been a Moonie for nearly three years. My parents had been afraid to mention to friends and members of their church that I had become a cult member. They were fearful of what others might think. Finally, though, my parents opened up. A prayer chain was started, and the church people began to pray for me around the clock.

In ten days I was out of the Unification Church.

What I didn't know then, but know now, was that two extremely potent forces were being deployed upon my life—love and prayer. If you learn nothing else from this book about how to deal with Moonies or members of other cults, know this: the power of God's love and the power of prayer are awesome.

This has been my story, the subject of my previous book, *Heavenly Deception,* and the scenario for the motion picture of the same title. Some of you may already know my story. Perhaps you've read the book or seen the movie or talked with friends about it.

Yet, while I truly hope that *Heavenly Deception* has had some impact upon people's lives, I am well aware of the limitations of both the book and film. Whenever I speak or lecture, there are dozens of questions from the audience. Every day, as I sort through my mail, I find some letter or note from a young person or from parents asking for advice. When I make personal appearances, there inevitably is someone, a mother usually, who wants help; her daughter or son has become a Moonie, she says, and I can see the hurt and confusion in her eyes. These are the questions and situations that my first book could not deal with. I hope that *What Do You Say to a Moonie?* can.

Being an ex-member of a cult does not make one an authority on his former comrades. Too often an ex-cult member mixes into his experiences strong doses of vengeance and hate. Often, his former colleagues are right when they accuse him of distorting the truth.

I certainly am not immune to these feelings.

However, my experience with the person of Jesus Christ has worked something of a miracle in my life. In examining myself as closely as possible, I find that I do not hate nor desire revenge against the Moonies.

By the grace of God I now see that hate and revenge are the weakest tools that Christians can use against the forces of this world. There will always be people who can out-hate me and out-debate me—but with Christ in my life no one can out-love me. Love is our greatest tool in dealing with the children of Satan. The love of God is the only thing which will change this world, the only thing which will ever change a Moonie.

Remember this, you who are parents and friends of cult members. As the dark hands of a cult have grabbed your loved one, you no doubt feel anger and hate rising up within you. What right do those wicked people have to whisk away my child, my friend?—that is your question. What right do those Moonies have to accost me with their flowers and requests for money in airports and on street corners? What right does the Unification Church have to buy up the industry and property of my town and invade my corner of the world with their false theology and vacant stares? These are your questions, and they're often expressed in a tone of vengeance. But remember, that hate and that anger welling up inside you are of Satan himself. And cults thrive on just that sort of caustic, vehement opposition. The only emotion a cult cannot deal with is genuine love.

Compassion is the key. If you expect to learn the answer to the question, "What do you say to a Moonie?" you must learn to love. You must learn to love the Moonies as God does.

A word of experience: I joined the Unification Church because the Moonies loved me and showed it; I left the Unification Church because I discovered that the Moonies' love for me was conditional—they loved me as long as I did what they wanted me to do. God's love is unconditional (John 13:35). As Christians, our love should be too.

A word of caution: loving the Moonies does not mean conceding to them. It does not mean buying their flowers or buying their theology. It does not mean allowing them to trample over the responsibilities of free speech. It does not mean allowing them to take our money. It does not mean giving them their way in places of government power.

What do you say to a Moonie? is a difficult question, one that requires a balance of love and realism. Hundreds of cults flourish in this world. Most of them seek to win our approval, our young people, and our money.

It is incumbent upon those of us who call ourselves Christians to have both a defense and an offense in dealing with cults.

TWO

What are the Moonies like?

Who are the Moonies? Where do they come from? What are they like? These are questions we need to ask; unfortunately, these are questions we *don't* ask.

Many people assume that kids in cults are sick, rebellious, or brainwashed. It is widely thought that cult members come from broken homes. It is believed that the young people who inhabit the cults received little or no church background as children. But none of this is necessarily true.

Many myths exist about the cults today. We are victims of sensational stories, many of which are founded upon exotic, bizarre cult incidents reported in the media. We know all too well the story of Jonestown, the sexual adventures of the Children of God, and tales of growing covens of witchcraft. Yet, few of us understand how one gets from here to there. We have no idea what a cult member is really like.

People in cults are real people. They grew up in real families. Usually they come to cults out of a real search for truth.

Don't get me wrong. I'm not defending the practices and beliefs of the cults. I'm trying to prevent us from a common failure—ignorance. As Christians we have a responsibility to be as informed as possible. We need to ask questions and get answers before we deal with the Moonies face to face.

They come from our churches.

If I introduced you to ten Moonies, you'd be surprised by what you found. Seven of those ten would at one time have been members of mainline denominational churches. In other words, they left us!

So we have little justification for pointing fingers. We can't very well talk about what's wrong with them until we determine what's wrong with us.

This point, too, is effectively used by the cults themselves. Cults argue that traditional churches are dying, and that they (the cults) are the rightful heirs to God's dispensation.

I'm not using this point to sling criticisms at the established church. I belong to the Christian church, and I believe in it. But this is what we're up against. This is what cults, indeed the Moonies, will throw back in our faces. Some 70 percent of their members once attended our churches. What went wrong?

They left us because we did not love them enough. Many Moonies left the Christian church because they needed to be loved. The Unification Church provided that love; the Christian church did not. It's a sad thing to report, but it's true. Often young people become disillusioned with the church they're a part of. Sometimes this disillusionment is the product of an excessive idealism—something the church can do nothing about. But often, it must be admitted, the disillusionment is grounded in fact: there *is* a lack of love in many churches; people often *are* at odds with each other; needs *are* frequently ignored by the church body.

They left us because they saw hypocrisy in us. In the movie *Heavenly Deception* there is a scene in a parking lot showing a Moonie handing a flower to the driver of a car. The driver, intimidated, presses a button and the window goes up, crushing the flower. As the car drives off, we read a sticker pasted on the back bumper—"Honk If You Love Jesus."

This, of course, is a symbol—a rather obvious one—of the contradiction and hypocrisy that people see in some Christians. Often, the Moonie receives not love but rejection from Christians. To many Moonies, the Christian church is filled with such examples, and thus Christianity is considered an "impure" faith.

(To be fair, the Unification Church also is subject to certain hypocrisy, not the least of which is "heavenly deception." But to most Moonies, the Unification Church is made up of pure, loving, well-meaning people.)

They left us because we diluted our theology and morality. Young people all over the world are looking for something to believe in. The intriguing thing about the Unification Church is how complex and demanding it can be theologically. Moonie theology is a theology that requires commitment.

How ironic it is that in recent years some Christian churches have watered down their faith and simplified their theology. In an effort to make Christianity easier to accept, they have reduced it to mush. In trying to make commitment to Christianity easy, these churches, in effect, require no commitment at all.

Being a Moonie requires sacrifice. It involves total commitment. And this is what many young people, deep down, really desire to do with their lives.

Who are the Moonies? Where do they come from? They come from our churches. They left us for something which they felt was more significant.

The Moonies are moral.

The next matter which might surprise you about the ten Moonies I would introduce to you is that they are all impeccably moral. They do not smoke, drink, do drugs, or involve themselves in sexually illicit behavior. Their personal morality is at least as good as most Christians', if not better.

It is not true that most Moonies are or were part of the drug culture. Moonies abhor the use of drugs—it goes against the grain of their theology. The same can be said of drinking and smoking.

Further, Moonies are extremely conservative when it comes to sexual matters. The Unification Church does not allow sexual immorality. Even when Moonies marry (in ceremonies conducted by the Rev. Moon), the union is sometimes not consummated for months, even years.

But remember, the fact that the Moonies are moral doesn't mean that they have a relationship with Jesus Christ. Although they appear to us to be such "good" kids, they aren't necessarily less dangerous, less evil. Don't forget that the devil can appear as an "angel of light" and seem quite beautiful and attractive.

God hates the sin, but loves the sinner. As Christians, we should hate the cult, but love the cult member.

Most Moonies are young and educated.
Over 80 percent of those who join cults are of college age at the time they join. Many Moonies, for example, are recruited right on the college campus. This fact has a further implication: namely, that most Moonies are well educated. Many have strong liberal arts backgrounds.

Of course, there are exceptions. I remember one Moonie who joined when he was just thirteen years old. His parents were in the process of a divorce when he first met the local Moonie group. His father gained custody of him and allowed him to visit the Unification Church regularly. Within months Mark moved into the Moonie center—with his father's permission!

There are some senior citizens in the Unification Church. Tom was many years past retirement and lived in New York City. While waiting in line at the local delicatessan, he met a young Japanese Moonie. She befriended him and walked him home. They visited again and again, and all the while Tom had no idea that she was a Moonie, a member of Sun Myung Moon's church. Over the weeks their friendship grew. Nearly every day she brought Tom food or flowers. When she asked him to attend a Unification Church workshop, he gladly accepted. Within a few weeks Tom not only joined, but he signed over his home to the cult —valued at more than $100,000. Tom was lonely and a Moonie filled his need. And look at the price he was willing to pay for it.

Sometimes parents of Moonies will join the church, often out of fear of losing their children. One woman in the Northeast, a divorcee, joined after two of her three children had become Moonies. Privately, she states that she doesn't agree with Unification Church doctrine (she is of Catholic background), but she endorses the group for her children's sake.

Nevertheless, the majority of Unification Church members are between the ages of eighteen and thirty. These are the Moonies you meet on the street. These are the Moonies whose parents call me and ask, "Why did this happen to our family? We took him to church!"

Perhaps we can learn a lesson here about the

Christian home, the Christian family. Just as we have said that the Moonies come from our churches, so we can say that the Moonies come from our homes. The blame is to be laid at the feet of parents as well as at the doorstep of the church.

The first thing that I'm made aware of as I talk with parents is that being a parent is not an easy thing. Raising children is difficult! But, you know, sometimes families take their Christianity for granted. When every member of the family is a Christian, sometimes it is assumed that everything will turn out all right. As a result, many Christian families never study their Bibles together or pray together outside the church.

When a young person from such a family encounters a Moonie group, he or she is bound to be impressed by the spiritual closeness of the group. In fact, the Moonies call themselves the "Family," and they pray together, study together, and grow together. No wonder young people—even Christian young people—think then that they've found the ideal.

There is a well-known seminary professor who has two sons who are Moonies. Most people are shocked to discover this, and many try to analyze the family to determine what went wrong. Certainly there were family faults involved, but let me suggest something else as well. Just whose families do you think Satan will try to destroy, anyway? Those whose lives he already controls? Of course not. Satan's power will be unleashed upon *Christian* families —those souls which have the most potential in serving God. Christian families are the targets of Satan's arrows. So as Christian parents we have to be strongly rooted in God's Word and closely knit together through prayer to withstand the wiles of the devil.

Many Moonies are Jewish.

Jewish families, too, are the victims of cults, especially the Moonies. About 20 percent of the Unification Church is made up of Jews. Often the Jewish convert was convinced that it was his ancestors that "murdered" Jesus and thus are particularly responsible for the state of the world today. There is a great deal of guilt imposed upon Jews by the Unification Church. One Jewish Moonie said to me that every time he looked in his hands he saw blood.

Articles have been written in several Jewish publications to inform the Jewish community of what is going on. A New York rabbi has begun a crusade to release young Jews from the entrapment of cults.

I find it interesting that so many Jewish young people are searching for truth. They, too, sidestep the established Christian church because they feel we don't care enough about them.

Moonies are not brainwashed.

Perhaps this is the most common misconception about the Moonies. Brainwashing—in the sense of a forced program of personality change and indoctrination—is not at all the rule in the Unification Church, and I doubt that you can verify any instances of it at all. There is a difference between brainwashing and persuasion. I can vouch for the fact that most Moonies choose the Unification Church of their own free will. I did. I'll admit that the persuasive powers of the Unification Church are considerable, that their theology is ingenious, and that the propaganda that is unloaded upon a Moonie is substantial. But force is not used and there are no special brainwashing "sessions" that a Moonie goes through in order to become a child of the Rev. Moon.

It is important to accept this truth if you are to deal with the Moonies in person. People who believe in the brainwashing theory sell short the strength and cleverness of the Unification Church. They are suggesting that the only way a reasonable person could possibly buy the claims of the Moonies is through force. They are saying that the power of the Unification Church is merely physical, not spiritual. Believe me, they are wrong! The Moonies are a spiritual power of this world and they have better ways of accomplishing their ends than by a technique as clumsy and obvious as brainwashing.

"But," you may ask, "what about the glassy-eyed, spaced-out look I see in the eyes of cult members?" I reply to you, "If you worked twenty hours a day, seven days a week, selling flowers in parking lots, you'd look like that too!" Visit a college campus during finals week sometime. You'll see a lot of people who look like that.

The brainwashing theory absolves people of

responsibility. *Ex-Moonies* often claim they were brainwashed. But what better way to relieve the guilt and embarrassment of making such a colossal mistake with one's life? "It was those evil cult leaders. I couldn't do anything about it!"

Churches claim that brainwashing techniques are pirating away young people from their fellowships. The implication is that nothing can be done and that there is no blame in us for what has happened.

Parents claim that their children have been brainwashed. "Why else would they want to leave home?" Such a response overlooks the obvious: that there were reasons for these children to seek something else and that there were tensions in the family unit, making the claims of the Unification Church quite attractive to them.

Christians would like to think that Moonies are brainwashed because then it relieves them of the responsibility of loving and caring for and witnessing to Moonies encountered on the street corner or in the airport;.

What happens to a young person who joins the Unification Church isn't much different from what happens to a young person who goes on a church's youth group retreat. Lots of teaching and lots of fellowship. Emotions run high; sleep is minimal. Lots of starch and little protein. Motivation levels skyrocket. The methodology, you see, is quite the same. The difference is that a youth group retreat lasts a weekend. The

Unification Church membership lasts for years —maybe a lifetime.

The point I'm trying to make is that cult members are not monsters. They're people, real people like you and me, and they've joined a cult for real reasons. Often these cult members are young people who have grand ideals about the world, teenagers who are confused about the turmoil of our culture and unsure of their own identity in a modern world.

Perhaps it seems as if I'm defending cults or standing up for the Unification Church. I am not. You'll see in forthcoming chapters that I am not. But the reason that we have a cult problem is that so few understand about the cults. So few bother to find out who cult members are and what they need. And that, in a nutshell, is the cult problem.

To bring this down to the most practical level, let's consider the story of a Moonie, a young girl named Julie.

Case study—Julie.

Julie was eighteen years old and a freshman at the University of Alabama when she joined the Moonies. It was a time of transition for Julie, and a time of decision-making. She wanted to major in sociology at school because she was concerned about the poverty that she had seen in the small towns and cities throughout Mississippi and Alabama. She wanted to help people who had needs; she wanted to work with poor black families and help them become strong and financially independent. Julie's father, however, had other ideas. He argued that sociology was an impractical major and that if Julie became a sociologist, she'd likely wind up as poor as the people she wanted to help. "I was confused," Julie says about that time in her life. "Fortunately, I didn't have to declare my major until the end of the year. I had some time to think it over."

In high school Julie had been extremely popular. She had been a cheerleader and was elected student body vice-president in her senior year. A strikingly attractive blonde, Julie had always had many boyfriends and dated frequently. Her grades were always good in high school, although Julie never had to work very hard for them—schoolwork came quite easily to her.

At home Julie's relationship with her parents had been a congenial one. She loved her mother and father, but felt that they were too strict with her. Julie was an only child and because of that she felt that her parents were overprotective of her. "I wanted them to trust me more," she says, "to give me more rope."

Their family was a religious family—they attended a Methodist church in town every Sunday—and Julie had worked in a Young Life group for two years. Yet, though they called themselves Christians, Julie had always sensed that something was missing in their home life together—something spiritual. Sometimes Julie had really deep thoughts about

God and eternal things, but she was afraid to express herself at home because she wasn't sure if her father, and especially her mother, ever thought about such things.

"It got rough during my senior year in high school," Julie recalls. "Rough at home, that is. I was getting into quarrels with Mom, and I didn't seem to get along with Dad very well." Julie had become sensitive to the issues of ecology and energy conservation through a school project in which she had participated; it bothered her that her parents were so wasteful and that her father hadn't properly insulated their house. Julie began to notice how many material possessions her parents owned, and it troubled her.

For all these reasons, going away to college was a relief, a newfound freedom, and an opportunity to explore her ideals and independence fully. Julie took up the idea of the sociology major with enthusiasm because it was her own idea, not her parents', and because it was something that no one expected an ex-cheerleader to do.

"By the time the spring semester rolled around, I was growing tired of the popularity bit," Julie reports, "and I began to realize that other things were more important than beautiful hair and a fair complexion. For the summer, I wanted to travel; Dad wanted me to work at a bank and earn money."

Just at that time a group of a dozen or so young people wearing white shirts and blouses and dark pants or skirts appeared on campus.

They were a community of some sort and claimed to be Christians working toward a unified, peaceful world. This One World Crusade held lectures in a building on campus. Out of curiosity, Julie attended.

The lectures, for the most part, were boring. There was a lot of dry historical material about the Bible and original man. Julie was mildly interested in the philosophy of personal sacrifice that the group espoused, but most of all it was its fresh perspective of Christianity that grabbed Julie's interest. That, and of course the group's open display of love.

"They were very close to one another, and they showed their love to me quite freely," Julie says. "Never in my church or home had love and compassion been so openly demonstrated."

Julie grew closer and closer to the group members, until she knew for sure that this was what she wanted for herself. Julie decided to join three weeks after the first lecture.

At this point Julie still knew very little about the group, except that they went by a different name—the Unification Church—and that they had some original, sensible thoughts about Christianity, history, and the future of mankind. Julie still was not sure who the Rev. Sun Myung Moon was nor how many people like herself belonged to the Unification Church.

"In June of that year I moved out of my dormitory room and moved in with the group. I dropped out of school, forfeiting my registration privileges for the next year. Many of my relationships with my college friends were severed, not so much because of anything I did, but because my friends couldn't understand why I was joining the Unification Church. When I joined, my first inclination was to call my parents in Mobile, but the leader of the group, John, told me not to."

As it is with most Moonies, Julie was warned that Satan would use any and all means to keep her from doing the work of God. Even her parents would be subject to evil influence, she was told. Julie waited two weeks before she informed her parents.

"When I did call, it was a bad, bad scene. Mom cried practically the whole time, and Dad was furious. Dad threatened to drive up to the University to get me, but I said that if he did, I'd run away. I tried to explain to them that I loved them and that I wasn't rebelling against them. This was just something I had to do, something I felt strongly about, a decision I needed to make on my own. I told them that I didn't see what the fuss was all about."

In the next few months Julie moved fully into the work of the Church. She sold flowers in shopping centers and raised money—sometimes as much as $250 a day. The group spent lots of time in prayer, and they studied the *Divine Principle* extensively. Usually Julie got only four or five hours sleep a night. The rest of the time was spent in prayer, study, or fund raising.

Living with the group was a sacrifice for Julie, but a sacrifice she wished to make.

When she joined the group in June, she had sold all of her record albums and had donated the money to the cult. Her many clothes had been given away to friends at the college, and many of her personal things—posters, pictures, nostalgic mementos—had been shipped home. While in the group Julie lived out of a suitcase. Other than a few books and a Bible, Julie owned very little.

In September, Julie was granted permission to arrange a meeting with her parents in Tuscaloosa. All activities of group members had to be approved by the group leader—in this case, John. John thought it might be helpful for Julie to see her parents again, to test her allegiance to the Church. It was important, however, that Julie meet her parents in a neutral place—not in hometown Mobile. Tuscaloosa was settled on and the arrangements were made.

Julie's mother speaks of her reactions at the rendezvous. "My daughter had lost weight. She looked thin and her hair was straggly. She didn't look healthy at all. There was a vacant look in her eyes, and I thought that maybe she had gotten involved with drugs. Strangely, Julie looked plain, and I guess that scared me the most because my little girl's never looked plain in her life. I wondered if she really was my daughter."

Julie says: "It was a little awkward meeting Mom and Dad again. I wanted them to know I was happy and doing what I wanted to do. I was working for the perfection of humanity, for ultimate salvation—I couldn't understand why they wanted me to stop it all and come home. I had been warned that Satan, no doubt, had gotten to Mom and Dad and they'd do just about anything to keep me from returning to the Church. I didn't think that they'd be tempted so easily. But when Daddy offered me a new car, one that I had always talked about when I was in college, I knew it was time to leave them to get back to the work of the Church and my friends who would love me and support me."

This is a painful place to conclude this story, but it's right that we do finish here, because this is the point at which many parents and Moonie children live today. Many families are torn by this very same pain.

This portrait is typical. There is no coercion, no brainwashing. Moonies live simple, moral lives. They work hard. They are extremely idealistic and live for the fulfillment of their ideals, ideals which Moon claims can be achieved. They are gradually taught that they must always be wary of the forces of Satan, and this leads them further into dependence upon the Church. Eventually the Church gets a Moonie to burn all his bridges behind him—to cut ties with parents, friends, job responsibilities, college, possessions. Ultimately the Unification Church is all that a Moonie has.

What can be done? How do we deal with the Moonies? What do we say to a Moonie?

Well, we have already taken the first step. We

have learned that a Moonie is a human being with needs and ideals and very intense emotions. Furthermore, we must remember that the Moonie we see on a street corner or in an airport is someone else's child.

MYTHS ABOUT THE MOONIES

1. Moonies never went to church as children.
Actually, most Moonies (approximately 70 percent) did grow up in established, mainstream churches.

2. Moonies come from the drug culture and many are addicts.
No, Moonies do not do drugs, and in fact abhor the drug culture. A high standard of personal morality is the trademark of a Moonie.

3. Moonies are ill-educated; many are dropouts.
Most Moonies have considerable education. If any are dropouts, they are *college* dropouts, and left school for the Unification Church, not for reasons of bad grades.

4. Moonies are involved in illicit sexual activity.
Nothing could be farther from the truth. The sexual union, in Moonie theology, is a particularly important matter. As a result, the Moonies abstain from sexual immorality. Even after Moonies are married (by the Rev. Moon), often the marriage is not consummated for months, even years.

5. Moonies are brainwashed.
Probably not. Indoctrinated, yes; brainwashed, no. What looks to some people as a brainwashed "look in the eyes" is often nothing more than a lack of sleep. You see the same look on a college campus during finals week.

6. All Moonies are young people.
Most are under thirty, it is true. But there are some over thirty, too. In fact, there are some senior citizens in the Unification Church.

7. Most Moonies were formerly affiliated with Protestant denominations.
As reported before, many Moonies once were involved in Protestant churches. But there are former Catholics and also many Jews in the Unification Church.

THREE

What do the Moonies believe?

Unification Church theology is a fascinating, sometimes outrageous, revisionism of the Christian faith. At times it appears remarkably compatible with Christianity, and indeed that's what the Unification Church leaders would like people to think. In reality, the theology is a gross distortion of Christianity, denying the deity of Christ and preempting the authority of the Scriptures.

Our consideration of Moonie theology will be brief and general. For one thing, the theology of the Unification Church is far too complex and extensive to be considered in one short chapter. Also, I believe that when it comes to dealing with a Moonie face to face, the subject of theology is overemphasized. It often becomes a smoke screen that hides real needs. What most cult members are searching for, it must be remembered, has more to do with love and sense of worth than it does with philosophy

33

and a clever theology. (More about this later.)
So it's important to view the matter of theology
from the proper perspective.

Still, there is much we can learn about
Moon's theology. It is interesting to see how
clever it is in adopting the structure of Christianity for its own purposes. First, it deserves
a few words of caution concerning the dangers
it poses.

The dangers of arguing theology with a Moonie.

When some people ask, "What do you say
to a Moonie?" they really mean, "What is the
Moonies' philosophy? What is their theology?
How can I effectively argue with them about
the truth?" Some especially zealous Christians
may hope to overwhelm a Unification Church
member with such irrefutable logic and such
airtight theological reasoning that the Moonie
will drop his flowers and candles right there in
the shopping mall and choose to follow Christ
instead of Moon. Some parents of Moonies,
with perhaps more justifiable motivations, wish
to use the keys of theology and philosophy to
free their sons or daughters from the prison of
the cult.

But there are great dangers in this approach
to the Moonies. Usually, Christians underestimate a Moonie's mastery of his own
theology. And Christians often overestimate
their own knowledge of Christian thought. We
forget that most Moonies are rather well
educated and that they have spent months

studying the *Divine Principle,* the Bible, and the teachings of the Rev. Moon. We forget that many of these cult members came from mainline churches and thus know well our side of the argument as well as their own.

Most of all, I should caution you concerning the "slipperiness" of Moon's theology. It is not an easy theology to pin down, for the following reasons:

1. The theology of the Unification Church is an eclectic mixture of dualism, deism, Eastern philosophy, and Judeo-Christian thought which is often presented in a biblical terminology that is deceptively Christian.

2. Moon's theology is often presented orally, when, as Richard Blake in *America* puts it, "there is no opportunity to look back to check consistency and realize that apples and oranges are being counted together rather easily."

3. Many Moonies are not aware of the *complete* Unification Church theology. (This was true in the case of Julie.) Theology is presented in a general fashion and any pointed questions are answered elusively. I know this from my own experience. As I spent more time in the Unification Church, I learned new facets of Unification theology that I had not been told at the beginning. So, when you talk with a Moonie, he or she may deny some of your claims, simply because he or she has not been informed of the complete theological system.

4. Moon's theology has a tendency to change from time to time. The doctrinal guide of the Unification Church, the *Divine Principle,*

has been revised several times since 1954. Since its inception, the Unification Church has gone through several phases in which it has readjusted its goals and aims. From a minor Oriental cult in the 1950s the Unification Church has grown into an international organization with not only spiritual, but political and economic goals as well.

5. Finally, consider the principle of "heavenly deception." Moonies are told to do and say anything which furthers the work of the Church. This extends to the point of being intentionally misleading or even dishonest. For example, in fund raising Moonies often pitch the line that they are collecting money for a drug center to rehabilitate addicts. The money they are given goes instead to the central organization of the Unification Church where it is used to purchase industry and real estate or to finance political front organizations on Capitol Hill. Again, in a discussion of theology a Moonie is not bound to complete truthfulness if the Church could benefit in some greater way from an untruth. If in a discussion with you, a Moonie sees a way of diffusing your opposition to the Church, he or she may quite easily say something that is not the true teaching of the Unification Church—all for the purpose of making you a friend rather than a foe.

There is one final reason why you should be wary of entering into a dialogue or argument with a Moonie over theology. *You may be overlooking the real need of that Moonie.* Although Unification Church theology is compelling and persuasive, my guess is that most Moonies become Unification Church members for emotional reasons, primarily love. The pattern is this (and it's been verified over and over): a young person is attracted to the Unification Church because it offers an emotionally comfortable environment—true friends and an open, unreserved expression of love. The Church becomes a family to the Moonie, a family wherein he or she has a place of significance. So you may be standing there in that airport arguing your head off over the meaning of Luke 22:70, and all the while what that Moonie young person really needs is to know that you love him or her. Sometimes it's just that simple.

The theme of Moon's theology.

The perfection of the human race is the ultimate goal of the Unification Church and the cornerstone of Moon's theological system. To state it simply, Moonies believe that there existed in the Garden of Eden a "trinity"—God, Adam, and Eve—which was intended to create the family of God's children, a perfect race. Of course, sin got in the way (Moonies believe that Eve was seduced by Lucifer), Adam and Eve were banished from the Garden, and God had to try it again, later.

One of the philosophies that the Unification Church borrows from is that of dualism—the division of all life into Good and Evil, the spiritual and the material. The failure of Adam and Eve created a cycle in human history of "battles" between the Good and the Evil, a cycle which began with Cain and Abel. Cain (Evil) triumphed over Abel (Good). Subsequently throughout history the Cain-type fought the Abel-type for supremacy.

It wasn't until the time of Jacob that the "Abel" gained the upper hand against the "Cain." You'll remember how Jacob repossessed the birthright from Esau and later wrestled with the Angel of the Lord. Moonies believe that Jacob was chosen by God at a turning point in history to father a nation which would bring about the perfecting of God's children.

Moon's theology divides human history into roughly 2000-year segments. The time from Adam to Jacob is approximately 2000 years; and if you measure 2000 years from the time of Jacob, you come to the era of Jesus Christ.

Jesus, too, was to bring about a perfect human race. Jacob had set it up for him to do so. But Christ did not marry. Moonies will be careful to say that Christ did not *fail,* yet, in Moon's theology, Jesus did not complete his primary mission. The opportunity was lost for the perfecting of the human race—at least for another 2000 years.

Now, the Unification Church has measured rather precisely these 2000-year segments of time. They are not really 2000 years at all, but are found to fall into a range between 1,917 years and 1,930 years. If you calculate the period of time when the next "Messiah" is due by adding 1,917 or 1,930 to the date of Christ's birth, you come up with the years 1917 and 1930. Furthermore, the Church is fond of quoting Bible verses that speak of the East, and it points to the fact that all the major religions have their origins in the Orient. The Unification Church concludes that the new "Messiah" will come from the Orient and will have been born between the years 1917 and 1930.

The Rev. Sun Myung Moon was born in what is now North Korea, in 1920.

The Unification Church believes that Moon is the Messiah come to earth to create a perfect race. This perfection is supposed to occur through the mass marriages he conducts and through a principle called *indemnity*. Indemnity is a means of paying God back for sins committed. An elaborate doctrine of "good works," indemnity not only demands that a person pay for his own redemption but that he or she also pay for the redemption of his or her ancestors who fell short. As this is accomplished, the human race will be perfected.

It is important to note that Moon's theology is based on the notion that the original sin was primarily sexual (Eve was seduced by Lucifer). "The root of man's sin stems from adultery," says the *Divine Principle*. As a result, the core of Unification Church theology has to do with sexual purity, marriage, and procreation. Even the significance of Moon himself is presupposed upon his ability to bring about a pure human race through marriage. It is up to him to correct what Adam and Eve ruined at the start. Thus Moonies call Moon and his wife the "True Parents."

Moon's theology has political implications, particularly in regard to the end times. The Unification Church identifies certain nations of the world as "good" and others as "bad." Communist nations, of course, are considered bad, Cain-type nations (Moon was held prisoner by Korean Communists early in his life). If Moon's efforts to perfect humanity do not succeed, the Abel-nations and the Cain-nations will go to war; this will be the final conflict between God and Satan. In the "Last Days" the nation of Korea will be the "Third Israel."

Simplified, this is the gist of Moon's theological system. But there are some specifics worth noting for the manner in which they conflict with Christian teaching.

Christianity and the Unification Church: How they match up.

The Bible and the Divine Principle. The *Divine Principle* is a 536-page work, composed by Moon's Korean followers sometime in the early 1950s. It is based on a vision of Jesus Christ that Moon claims to have had in 1936. It claims to be the "new, ultimate, final truth." Moonies study the *Divine Principle* as if it were the Holy Scriptures, and while they don't deny the Christian Bible a place in their theology, the Word of God is used as a source secondary to the *Divine Principle*. The Bible, moreover, is usually considered for its historical insight and not for spiritual guidance. Still, most Moonies will say that they believe in the Bible and accept its teachings.

The *Divine Principle* is really a principle of creation: all reality is dualistic: good-bad, positive-negative, masculine-feminine. It operates in the manner I have already described: God sought to form a trinity with Adam and Eve; and for the perfection of mankind to be accomplished, God will have to form a trinity with Moon and his wife.

Besides placing the Word of God in a position inferior to the words of men, the conflict between the Bible and the *Divine Principle* ought to be obvious. The *Divine Principle* is extra revelation; it is not canonical, and it has not been accepted by the Christian church. In many ways the *Divine Principle* contradicts the Bible (however, some Moonies can be very clever in arguing that it does not).

Jesus Christ and the Rev. Sun Myung Moon. The Moonies declare that Moon is Christ even as Jesus was Christ. We all are sons of God. Jesus was one with God, even as we all can be one with God.

But traditional Christian teaching is that Jesus was God made flesh. He was *the* Son of God. He was *the* Christ, *the* Messiah.

Moonies believe that Jesus' death on the cross was not a first choice but a last resort. They believe that Jesus should have lived for us, not died for us. When Jesus died, his mission on earth was ended, so they believe.

Furthermore, the Unification Church denies the reality of the physical resurrection.

Of course, the Christian church believes that Jesus died, was buried, and rose again from the dead, and that this was God's redemptive plan.

Salvation and Indemnity. The doctrine of indemnity in Unification Church theology appears to be something like the doctrine of "good works" that Christians refute as being unbiblical. In the Moonie system of thought, belief in redemption through the cross, baptism, and holy communion are examples of "lesser indemnity." In any case, "salvation by grace through faith" is not much proclaimed in the Unification Church, and it is difficult to see how grace can play much of a role in a Moonie's thought system as long as he or she does not believe that Jesus Christ should have died on the cross nor that he physically rose again from the dead.

Christianity and the Unification Church. Some people call the Unification Church a "pseudo-Christian" cult because it often appears so compatible with Christian truth. The Moonies would like people to think that they are a legitimate faction of the Christian church. As we have seen, Moon's theology appropriates Christian teaching to its own ends and reinterprets Christian truth to support the suppositions of the Unification Church. Perhaps this is the most dangerous of all cults for this very reason: that it tries to "rewrite" Christian truth, and in the process confuses and attracts many people who are casually acquainted with Christianity.

It is significant that even the most liberal and tolerant of Christian organizations, The National Council of Churches, refuses to recognize the Unification Church as a legitimate Christian church. According to the NCC's Commission on Faith and Order, "continuity with the Christian faith" requires these affirmations:

1. That Jesus of Nazareth is the Christ, the eternal Word of God made flesh.
2. The life, death, and resurrection of Jesus are the ground and means of the salvation of persons and of the whole creation.
3. The triune God—Father, Son, and Holy Spirit—has acted as Creator, Redeemer, and Sanctifier identifying with the suffering and need of the world and is effectively saving it from sin, death, and the powers of evil.
4. There is an essential relationship between faith in the saving work of the triune God and obedient response of the believing community.

The NCC concludes that "the Unification Church is not a Christian church because its doctrine of the nature of the triune God is erroneous; its Christology is incompatible with Christian teaching and belief; and its teaching on salvation and the means of grace is inadequate and faulty." The NCC study further concludes that "the claims of the Unification Church to Christian identity cannot be recognized because the role and authority of Scripture are compromised in the teachings of the Unification Church; revelations invoked as divine and normative in *Divine Principle* contradict basic elements of Christian faith; and a 'new, ultimate, final truth' is presented to complete and supplant all previously recognized religious teachings, including those of Christianity."

For conservative Christians this pronouncement of the NCC commission is significant, for if they, the most accepting of Christian groups cannot view Moon's theology as valid Christian teaching, how much more should conservative Christians, fundamentalists and evangelicals, resist the distortions of Christianity that the Unification Church works throughout the United States and the world?

What is a cult?

So the Unification Church cannot lay claim to the Christian faith. We are calling it a cult—but what really is a cult? I have had to work out a definition of the word "cult" that could be understood by a layman like me.

First, you have to recognize that you get confused if you try to define a cult according to methodology. The reason for this is that many Christian groups use methodology that cults use: not brainwashing, necessarily, but propaganda, persuasion, indoctrination, etc. We have seen how much like a youth group retreat the program of initiation into the Unification Church really is.

No, a cult must be defined according to its theology—what it believes. I have discovered five points that I believe define a cult. Any group that holds *most* of these characteristics may be classified as cultic.

1. Presence of a new prophet or messiah that the rest of the body of Christ does not receive. His or her word is accepted as ultimate authority. Followers (disciples) are encouraged to trust this authority to the extent of total dependency.
2. The recording of new revelation that takes equal if not superior position to the Bible. Also, changing the Word of God to adapt it to a particular doctrine.
3. A redefinition of the role and person of Jesus Christ.
4. A general rejection of the group by the whole society—even the non-Christian element.
5. A group composed of a relatively small number of people.

The key word in the first point is authority. God has taught us to depend upon him. Yet, interestingly, the Christian is not absolved from personal responsibility. The more we depend on God, the more we are able to handle our responsibilities, to make wise decisions about matters in everyday life.

But responsibility is something that many people are afraid of. Many of us are glad to let others take over our lives so that we can be released from responsibility. Many find cult life satisfying for this reason. This is another reason why brainwashing has been overemphasized: too many people *want* to grant control of their lives to others—brainwashing isn't necessary.

The second point is the trickiest. So many Christians abuse Scripture by misinterpreting it or reading into it that when a cult does the same it's hard to discern. Just remember that the Bible is the final authority, and don't be afraid to rely on the teachings of those Christians who have gone before us: Calvin, Luther, Aquinas, Augustine, etc.

Then, what is the true role and person of Jesus Christ? Traditional Christian teaching states that Jesus Christ is the full and complete revelation of God to man. (No further revelation is necessary.) The biblical Jesus is represented as the Son of God, God himself made flesh.

The last two cult characteristics mentioned help differentiate cults from major world religions and sects. World religions are represented by large numbers of people. Sects are often heretical in regard to the Christian faith, but they are socially accepted. Cults are neither large nor socially accepted.

WHAT DO YOU SAY TO A MOONIE?

Gradually, we are answering this question. We know now what a Moonie is like and basically what he believes. However, as much as we learn about the Moonies, we must not assume that we know them better than they know themselves, or that we understand what they believe better than they do.

Above all, our interactions with the Moonies must be marked by respect, love, and grace.

FOUR

What else should I know about the Moonies?

As I travel, lecture, and appear on TV discussing the Moonies, many excellent questions are put to me concerning the cult. Some of these I've collected and use in my lectures. These questions, reprinted in this chapter, may help fill out your knowledge about the Moonies, the way they live, and what they're doing on street corners, in shopping malls, and in airport terminals.

How many Moonies are there?
Various Unification Church estimates range from 50,000 on up. However, a figure of this sort is hard to document. Furthermore, the Unification Church tends to inflate its figures, counting anyone who has expressed interest in the Church as a member or associate member.

Once I was talking with the mother of one of the Unification Church leaders. She was an associate member of the Unification Church, and thus would be counted in its membership estimate. She was of Catholic background, I knew, and, my curiosity piqued, I asked, "Do you really believe in the Unification Church?"

"Of course not," she replied. "I only say I do—to keep my son."

I estimate that there may be only 7,000 Moonies in America. If they seem to be more numerous to you, it may be you've got them mixed up with other cult groups. Also, Moonies tend always to "be on the job." They sleep very little and work very hard. Consequently, there may appear to be more of them than there really are.

Every so often Moon conducts a "mass marriage." What is the idea behind that?
Every five or so years, Rev. Moon conducts a mass marriage. The first was performed with twelve couples. Each subsequent ceremony has wedded a greater number of couples, and a significant number, at that. These later ceremonies have married couples numbering 144, 777, and 1800; and in 1981, Moon will conduct another mass marriage which, at the time of this writing, is estimated to number 843. (This last figure was supposed to have been 5000; perhaps that many couples could not be found.)

The purpose of all this is theological. As we have already mentioned, the thrust of Unification Church theology is that of human perfection and the union of God's people on earth. Adam and Eve failed in that Eve was seduced by Lucifer; also, the Unification Church believes they consummated their union together before they were "mature." The original sin was sexual sin. To correct that, Moon must create a perfect race of people—the offspring of the couples he marries. Moonie couples, then, will fulfill what Adam and Eve failed to do; their children will be born "innocent," that is, without original sin.

The ceremony is called "the blessing." Moon decides who will marry whom, and he often mixes races, nationalities. To marry a Korean is considered a high honor in the Unification Church. Moon also decides how soon after the ceremony the marriage is consummated. Some couples have waited as long as three years. Moon tends to separate couples right after the ceremony and send them off in opposite directions.

Do the Moonies, like certain other cults, commit violent acts?
No, violence is totally out of character with Moon's theology and Unification Church practice. Kidnapping is unheard of. The only occasion where force has been used has been after a Moonie has been kidnapped by parents or a deprogrammer. Sometimes, then, Moonies will forcibly "recapture" one who is undergoing deprogramming.

Do you recommend deprogramming?
No. It often doesn't work. In cases of deprogramming that I'm familiar with, nearly 50 percent return to the cult. And once deprograming has occurred, it becomes even more

difficult for a cult member to leave a cult.

Deprogramming presupposes that brainwashing has taken place. As I've already mentioned, I don't think that brainwashing is the method of the Unification Church. And deprogramming a person who has not been brainwashed can be dangerous to that person.

Moreover, I would think that Christians could have ethical problems with using deprogramming as a method to win back a cult member. It is, perhaps, a tempting alternative, especially to some parents who are desperate, but upon closer examination you begin to realize that it should not be considered at all.

Is it common for members to leave the Church of their own accord, as you did?
Many Moonies leave the Unification Church of their own free will. In fact, the turnover is very high. Some estimates have it that one-third of the membership leaves the Unification Church every two years. I think that figure may be higher. In short, there is hope that Moonies will eventually leave the cult and lead normal lives.

How much money do the Moonies raise by selling flowers or candles?
You'd be surprised! In my experience, for a Moonie to raise $100 or less a day would be a poor return. Average return would run about $200 a day. Some Moonies have been able to raise $1000 or more in a single day!

If you assume that the average figure is $200, and if you assume that about 1,000 Moonies are out selling every day (a conservative figure, given the Unification Church's estimate of a total 50,000+ Moonies in the movement), then you realize that the Unification Church is taking in $200,000 every day. A million dollars every five days. Only a small portion of this money is used for expenses—food, lodging, etc. (Remember, the Moonies lead a simple life.) The rest of the money goes to Moon and his vast economic enterprises.

Are you suggesting that the Unification Church is heavily invested?
I'm not suggesting it—I'm saying it! The aims of the Unification Church extend to the economic and political realms as well as the spiritual.

The Unification Church is active mostly in New York and California business and real estate. But just recently they purchased over a million dollars' worth of real estate in Alabama, along the Gulf, and they've "invaded" the fishing port of Gloucester, Massachusetts, as well as bought up a substantial portion of that town's lobster industry.

The extensive real estate holdings of the Unification Church figure into the Church's future goals. Moon intends that someday he will be able to establish Moonie communities, little utopias, throughout the United States. The plan is that the living conditions of these communities will be so desirable that everyone else will want to get in. To achieve his goal, Moon has tentative projects designed to build schools and seminaries (some of this is already going on) to educate Moonies in science and the fine points of Unification theology.

Is everyone on the street corner who tries to sell me something a Moonie?
Absolutely not!

Street sales, while often not pleasant work, can be financially rewarding. If you are in the right place (busy parking lot, airport, or intersection) with the right product (flowers, candy, peanuts... impulse items), anyone can do well—no matter what his or her spiritual affiliation is.

Few people with conventional jobs can claim the per-day income of most street fund raisers. So some people get involved in street sales just to make money and really have no religious motivation at all.

Usually, those who are selling for cult groups will dress reasonably well, and have a conventionally acceptable appearance. The best salesman knows that if his customers are turned off by his appearance the sale will be lost. So don't think the organization is reputable just because the person looks reputable! That's just good salesmanship.

The converse of that is true as well. A person who appears shabby is not necessarily in a cult. In fact, that is usually a good indicator that he's in "the business" totally for himself.

Hare Krishna devotees used to appear publicly with their heads shaved, in their ritual cosmetics, and in flowing saffron robes. Their sales (especially in airports) dramatically increased when the men began to wear wigs and business suits. The women, although not stylish, changed to a more puritan image—long skirts, no make up, hair tied back. Some people say they don't see Hare Krishnas as much as they used to. Actually they're there, but just not so noticeable.

Another distinguishing factor of cult salesmen is that they'll usually try to sell their product in the name of a "good cause," rather than selling for the simple merit of the product: "Would you buy a flower to help feed hungry children?" or "We're selling candy to help support mission work."

And watch the holidays! More than once have cultists been discovered wearing Santa Claus suits at Christmas or patriotic costumes on July 4th. Their sales pitch will often be geared to the season. Don't underestimate the cleverness of these people.

Of course, rarely do you find someone who tells you the whole truth about "where the money goes." Few will identify themselves in terms you are familiar with (as Moonies or Hare Krishnas). There are several sub-organizations within all of these groups with much less obvious names. Some even sound "official."

The Unification Church was severely reprimanded in Atlanta for selling Girl Scout cookies. They purchased the excess cookies after that year's drive and began to market them. Citizens of Atlanta might have thought they were supporting the Girl Scouts by buying the product clearly marked Girl Scouts of America—but the funds were feeding Unification Church coffers.

Rarely do cult salesmen carry around literature to give you further information about their group. They depend on impulse buying, rather than giving you literature in hopes that you'll contribute later.

In summary, the best indicators that the person trying to sell you something is from a cult are:

1. Clean-cut appearance (rarely shabby, but there are exceptions).
2. Raising money for an organization (not selling flowers just for the sake of business).
3. Quick sale (most reputable organizations have literature and means of receiving your donation later).

Since many reputable organizations raise some of their funds by street or door-to-door sales —how can I tell the difference?
In most areas, door-to-door salesmen are required to wear clearly visible identification tags. Any reputable group will attempt to abide by local ordinances. If you don't know the person who approaches you, ask to see his ID tag. If he doesn't have one, you should be very careful about contributing—he may not be telling you the truth!

If he does have an ID, but it's for an organization you are not familiar with, then ask for literature and an address to which you can send a donation later. If he says he is fund raising for specific activities (orphanages, youth centers, mission work), ask for the exact location of such work. Remember, you don't have to donate right then. If it is worthy of your donation, your subsequent research will bear that out and you can donate later. If it proves to be a less than creditable organization, then you are wiser for the experience and can warn your family and friends.

Don't ever be afraid to ask a direct question. "Are you a member of the Unification Church?" (or any other group that you might suspect), is the best way I know to find out a fund raiser's affiliation. Rarely will he deny his movement, but it's still not foolproof.

If you are in an area where solicitation is prohibited (apartment complexes, shopping center parking lots, and neighborhoods) and you are solicited, what then? Will you be less than Christian if you report them?

No! Your church group has to abide by the laws, and so does *everyone* else's. You are also doing a service to those who may be more naive—those who might unquestioningly support the solicitor. Furthermore, you are not being cruel to the solicitor. You should stand against his organization, but not him personally. Differentiate your love and concern for him as a child of God from your objection to the organization he represents. God hates the sin, but still loves the sinner. Do likewise.

Further, don't be intimidated into donating. Some will make you feel guilty because you don't support their cause. But my contention is this: If you are giving all that you should in your own church, no one should be able to shame you into giving more.

If you want to support orphanages, most churches either directly sponsor or at least contribute to reputable orphanages. Earmark your donation for orphanages as you drop your offering in the plate on Sunday. You can be sure that your church will honor your request.

The same is true for drug rehabilitation programs, mission work, youth groups, relief for the poor and aged. Your church either already supports groups in these areas or will channel your money to a worthwhile organization.

In other words, for the responsible Christian, there is never any excuse for taking a chance. If the person who solicits you is not a personal acquaintance, or if you are not personally acquainted with the *specific* project or organization for which he is raising money, don't take a chance with an impulse contribution. If you feel the cause is worthy of your contribution, it will stand up to your investigation. That way, you will never lose.

Finally, discover the ways in which your church is doing similar work. You'll probably feel more confident of a ministry that your church already supports.

How should my church or community respond to the threat of the cults?
Recently churches and whole communities

have been confronted with the cult problem.

Not long ago a church in Dallas, Texas, contacted me. Early one Sunday morning a young man had walked into their worship service and responded to the invitation. He told the pastor he was a member of the Unification Church, but that he wanted out and had no place to go.

This church and I began to deal with this young man. A family took him in and found him a job. Several people within the church began to counsel him in an attempt to steady him spiritually. But a few days later he disappeared, much to the disappointment of the church. Many continued to pray for him.

Several weeks later a church in Lubbock told me a similar story. I began to put the two stories together and discovered that it was the same young man.

The immediate suspicion, of course, was that this young person was taking advantage of churches' hospitality and money, and that perhaps he should be turned out.

What should a church do in such a situation? It's a difficult problem to solve. On the one hand, it is wrong for a cult member to take advantage of churches, and certainly it is undesirable that churches support a cult even indirectly through such a person. (In some cases, money may be flowing from the church through the cult member into the cult.)

Nevertheless, such a young person has real spiritual and emotional needs. This young man, for instance, needed to know the love of Christ.

And what better place to help a Moonie than right in the midst of a church fellowship!

Remember, a Moonie needs to see something greater in us Christians than what he or she sees in the Unification Church. What happens when he or she comes to us (regardless of the motivation) and we respond by turning the Moonie out? Our action merely confirms the teaching of the cult.

I agree that we need to be wary of cult members in our midst. I agree that some discipline may be required. We do need to be firm. But we should strive to find ways to protect ourselves against the abuses of the cults *while at the same time loving and praying for the individuals within the cults.*

Then, too, there are whole communities which have been invaded by cult groups. Recently the Unification Church set up operations in the small Massachusetts town of Gloucester—and the Moonies have virtually taken over the fishing industry there. What can be done in such a case?

Communities are different from churches in that they are not composed entirely of Christians. Response to the cults becomes more a matter of civil propriety than spiritual concern. This is not to say that prayer and love are not applicable—indeed they are—but rather that there are other principles at work too.

The first advice I have is, "Be careful." Legal restrictions of cult activities in towns and cities can backfire. If we restrict the religious freedoms of a single group, those restrictions are likely someday to be applied to our own religious group. So we shouldn't panic and in the search for immediate solutions enact something which could forfeit a basic American freedom. Besides, any unfair laws would be overturned in the courts—and it may give the Unification Church (or other cult) opportunities for free publicity and newly won legitimacy.

Perhaps a community can restrict the fund-raising activities of groups. But here again we have to take care that by prohibiting fund raising of certain religious groups, we aren't restricting the activities of legitimate groups, such as the Girl Scouts, Boy Scouts, civic clubs, and other community groups. Still, if a community does not have written guidelines on fund raising, then some should be established.

FIVE

Why do I feel defensive toward the Moonies?

Rush hour traffic was the last place I expected to meet one.

Stopped at an intersection, I saw a young lady walking car to car, obviously trying to sell something. "Probably a Moonie," I thought. She was heading in my direction, but I was hoping the light would change before she got to me.

She was at the car ahead of me. A knot developed in my stomach. I would have to roll my window down and talk with her.

Wouldn't that light ever change?

She looked pleasant enough. But something about her approach threatened me and made me afraid. I found myself growing angry. "Why should I have to talk with her?" I thought. "If I want what she has, I'll go looking for it. She has no right . . . ."

How silly. A grown man intimidated by a wholesome-looking, innocent young girl. Still, I grew more uncomfortable as she came closer.

The car ahead of me had bought whatever it was she was selling. She immediately set her eyes and smile on me. Then she *ran* up to my car and leaned down toward the window.

"Sir?" she began.

I glanced up at the light. *Still* red.

Once again, in her feminine voice, "Sir... uh, excuse me, sir?"

There had to be some way out. Still looking straight ahead, both hands on the steering wheel, I made a fatal mistake. I glanced at her. She immediately caught my eyes and, thus, my attention. Still I made no move to roll down my window.

To my amazement, she said something that I'll never forget. "I'm not a Moonie," she proclaimed, somehow knowing that would make a difference to me.

But how did she know I used to be a "Moonie" myself? Surely, it was not *that* obvious. I didn't have it written on me anywhere, and I knew that she didn't know me from Adam. Why would she tell me something like that?

By this time I was rolling down my window. Before I had a chance to say a word, she had pulled a tabloid-size newspaper from under her arm and pushed it into my face. She said something about "youth."

The first thing that caught my eye was the emblem on the banner of the paper—a hammer and sickle. Communist! But, why would a Communist tell me that she is not a Moonie? My head was spinning.

She had already started into her pitch. Of course, she asked me to buy the paper, or at least *donate* to her "youth group." I wasn't so interested in communism, although it seemed paradoxical that her communism didn't threaten me. But, one question had to be asked.

Thank goodness, that light was *still* red.

"Why did you tell me that you weren't a Moonie?" I asked, obviously interrupting her well-rehearsed monologue.

Somewhat confused, she honestly replied, "People won't talk to me as long as they think that I'm a Moonie. I guess people are afraid of them." Pausing for a second, and then in a more reflective tone she added, "Once people find out that I'm a Communist, they'll argue with me all day long. But I guess people don't know how to defend their faith."

She hit the nail on the head. "I guess people don't know how to defend their faith." Sometimes the truth hurts.

The light changed . . . and so did my life.

God spoke to me loudly in that incident. I realized that not everyone selling things at intersections (or airports) is a Moonie. But more important, the young Communist girl helped me isolate the major problem concerning cults.

Cults are not the problem; they are the *result* of the problem. And more often than not, the problem lies within us as Christians. In that incident the problem was not whether that girl was a Communist or a Moonie. The problem was that I was afraid of her because I felt she was going to force me to defend my faith.

So many people who call themselves Christians cannot even explain their faith, much less defend it when put in a position to do so. When we can't defend our faith, our only option is to either ignore the situation, be rude, or stand aloof. In none of those options does Jesus Christ shine through.

Much of the reason that 70 percent of the people who call themselves Moonies come out of Christian backgrounds is that they too did not know how to defend their faith. When challenged, all they could do was crumble. It is estimated that 90 percent of the young people today who call themselves Christians get one hour or less of Bible study each week.

Would you fly in an airplane piloted by a man who had studied flying only one hour each week? Would you go into a building designed by an engineer who had studied only one hour per week? My point is that a lot of the reason that people join cults is that they never really understood the Word of God in the first place.

Many people who join cults are sincerely looking for the truth, but somehow they never saw it in us. And when one of these cultists meets us in the streets and finds that we are afraid of them, well, what kind of message does that leave?

Again, the problem is often not the cult itself, but the cult is the result of the problem; namely, that there are Christians who have known the Lord for years and years but have never gotten beyond the stage of being spoon-fed. Like infants, they are defenseless and totally vulnerable.

When people ask me, "What can I say to a Moonie?" I always answer, "I cannot tell you what to say." What one says must come from his experience in the Word of God. There are no pat answers when you confront someone from a cult. Each cult member is an individual with needs and questions. Unless he sees in us the answers, he will always walk away victorious.

If you intend to be harsh and judgmental, then there is no need of saying anything. The non-Christian world has been harsh and judgmental toward him already. He doesn't need a Christian to do that.

Remember, too, that your actions speak loudly. Rolling up the window rudely in the face of a Moonie speaks of weakness or fear. Being gruff often only confirms in their minds that we do not know God. But if a powerful God lives in your life, there will be no need to cower.

Our piety often oozes out when we deal with Moonies. A lot of us ignore them as they run along beside us in a parking lot trying to sell us flowers. This often leaves the impression that we think we are better than they are, or at least that we are "above" dealing with them. Yet, have I not read somewhere that we *all* have sinned and fallen short of the glory of God? Then what are we doing on a pedestal? Something, too, comes to mind about being saved by grace rather than works. Could someone who acts as if he really doesn't care really know God?

I don't bring up these points to criticize harshly, but only to turn a mirror on us to let us look at ourselves clearly. In learning what to say, we first have to look at what we are already saying. From there we can begin to change.

Realize, too, that what you say will be for naught if the Holy Spirit is left out. All of the words in the world never saved anybody outside of the power of the Holy Spirit. If your attitude is wrong, the Holy Spirit won't be able to use even the best-planned words.

Our defensiveness toward the Moonies is often the result of a lack of confidence in our own faith. And going out to attack the Moonies does little to solve the problem. I sincerely feel that the problem and the solution are all in the same place: the church—in other words, those of us who call ourselves Christians.

Yes, there are many problems in the church today. But all of the solutions are there, too. If we worked on solving our internal problems, many of the external problems, like cults, would dissipate. For where would cults get their new members and money if we were growing mature Christians within our own church fellowships?

SIX

What do you say to a Moonie?

We have learned a little of what Moonies are like, and we understand the rough outline of Moon's theology. We have added to our knowledge certain answers to questions concerning the organization and practices of the Unification Church. In the last chapter, we have examined our own defensive feelings toward cult members. Only now can we legitimately ask the question, "What do you say to a Moonie?"

MAKING CONVERSATION
We all have different dispositions and different ways of relating to people. Any "formula" for conversing with cult members needs to be personalized. But you might consider the following suggestions as a model for your own personal approach.

1. Don't be afraid to say no. You don't want to support the cult, therefore you won't want

69

to buy anything from a cult member. You can say no and still manage to engage that person in conversation.

2. *Ask them questions about their "cause."* If they claim to be Christian, then ask them about their relationship with Jesus Christ or about their conversion experience. You'll often find that they'll open up to you when they don't feel threatened by you. Be honest and genuine in your questioning, and listen closely to them.

3. *Don't be afraid to say, "I don't know."* If you don't know an answer to a question, or if you're not sure, admit that you don't know. You might add, "But I know someone who does. Would you like to talk with him (or her)?" No one expects you to know all the answers. Point the cult member to a source where the answer can be found.

4. *Express your humanness—that you are sinful and need salvation.* Many cults demand perfection from their members, and it becomes refreshing to some of them to meet an individual who is less than perfect, yet still secure in his or her faith. Don't let your faith become phony, a front, an act. Don't try to be something you aren't. God accepts us *as we are.* Share this with a cult member.

5. *Be hopeful and cheerful.* You'd be surprised how far a smile will go with someone who is searching for God.

6. *Try to be on the offensive rather than the defensive.* You shouldn't have to prove yourself to them; they're the ones trying to sell *you* something, remember? It is their task to prove

themselves worthy of your donation. Don't let them intimidate you by their attitude, "I am more spiritual than you are."

7. *You might ask what the cult member's parents think about his or her involvement in the cult.* Whatever the cultist's answer (and it usually will be that his or her parents approve of the cult, even though it often isn't true), offer to pay for a phone call to the parents right there on the spot. *Don't* give the person the money —place the call yourself. Usually he or she will turn you down. But if you do get through to the cultist's parents, you'll be putting that person in touch with the people who can most help him or her. Wouldn't you want someone else to do that if it were your child who had joined a cult?

8. *Buy the cult member a cup of coffee.* By this you are saying, "I care about you even though I don't agree with you." Use this time as an opportunity to talk about your own faith in Jesus Christ.

TALKING THEOLOGY
This is a rare opportunity—the chance to share Jesus Christ with a cult member on a conversational level. Most of the time, your contacts with cult members won't get beyond the stage of business: solicitation and transaction. If you do get to this point where the conversation has been opened and the relationship is comfortable, you should thank God for the opportunity and ask for grace and compassion with which to continue.

If you intend to guide the conversation to theological matters, what should you do?

First, prepare yourself mentally:

1. Relax.
2. Concentrate on listening carefully.
3. Think about what this person needs.

Second, remember that you are no expert. Treading theological waters is risky. You must avoid debate. In a debate, the better debater wins, not necessarily the better cause.

Third, focus on the essentials of the Christian faith. Your purpose at this point is not to prove the other person wrong, but to assert the central claims of Christianity. You should not try to prove that Christianity is true; rather, you should define what Christianity is and declare that you have accepted it by faith.

Finally, don't feel intimidated by your lack of knowledge concerning other cults or other religions. I used to think that if I intended to defend my faith in Jesus Christ against the claims of various cults and religions, I would have to know everything about each of these groups to be effective. I always felt inferior in certain situations, especially with Jehovah's Witnesses, Mormons, Hare Krishnas, and members of The Way International. Did I have to become an expert in the theological teachings of each of these groups in order to effectively uphold my Christian witness?

I don't think so. As Christians there are

certain matters of belief we all have in common. These are the essentials of our faith, and whether we are Methodist, Nazarene, Baptist, or Episcopalian we all share this same fundamental Christianity. Details may differ, but the basics are the same. If a person does not hold to these essential points, we may legitimately question his Christianity. If a religious group member quotes the Bible to you, measure what he says against these essential tenets of the Christian faith. If his statements don't coincide with these basics, the group cannot be considered Christian.

I. Jesus.

This is crucial. Many groups acknowledge Jesus in some way, but will glibly shove him aside in their theology. A Christian acknowledges (a) Jesus Christ's divinity, and (b) his virgin birth.

Divinity. Many cult groups, and especially the Unification Church, deny that Jesus was God. Christians claim that he was God; traditional Christian theology asserts that Jesus was God; and the Bible affirms that Jesus was God.

1. Jesus himself claimed to be divine. "I and my Father are one," Jesus said (John 10:30). (Also, Luke 22:67-70; John 10:37, 38; John 12:45; John 14:7-10.)
2. The Apostles claimed Jesus was divine. Peter said to Jesus, "Thou art the Christ,

the Son of the living God" (Matthew 16:16). (Also, John 1:1, 2; Colossians 2:9; 1 Timothy 3:16; Hebrews 1:3.)
3. God the Father said that Jesus was divine. "This is my beloved Son, in whom I am well pleased" (Matthew 3:17). (Also, Matthew 17:5; John 8:18; 1 John 5:9.)
4. Evil spirits confessed Jesus' divinity. (See Matthew 8:29; Mark 1:24; Luke 4:41; Acts 19:15.)

Virgin Birth. Surprisingly, several cults claim that Jesus' birth was merely a natural one, with an *earthly* father and mother. This is often done to legitimize one of the "new Christs" who has earthly parentage.

1. Jesus was not the son of Joseph. (See Matthew 1:18, 25; Isaiah 7:14.)
2. Jesus was the Son of God. (See John 1:14; 1 John 4:9.)

II. Jesus' death and resurrection.

Many cult groups consider the death of Christ to represent a victory for Satan and the failure of Jesus, often as some blunder that voided God's redemptive plan. The Scriptures clearly refute these mistaken beliefs. The Bible declares that Jesus' death was both *foretold* and *necessary for salvation.* Furthermore, it suggests that without the resurrection, Christianity is in vain.

1. Jesus' suffering was foretold. (See Isaiah 53:4-6; Isaiah 53:12.)
2. Christ's death was essential for our redemption. (See Ephesians 2:16; Colossians 2:13-15; 1 Corinthians 1:17.)
3. The resurrection of Jesus is the cornerstone of the Christian faith. "If Christ be not risen, then is our preaching in vain . . ." (1 Corinthians 15:14). Also, 1 Corinthians 15:14-23.)

III. Salvation by grace, not works.

Many cult groups have systems of redemption that are some form of "good works." The Moonies, for example, have "indemnity." Christians believe, and the Bible states very clearly, that our salvation comes through the grace of God, not by the efficacy of our good works, indemnity, or any other human work.

1. Salvation by grace. "But we believe that through the grace of the Lord Jesus Christ we are saved . . ." (Acts 15:11). (Also, Romans 3:24; Romans 5:15; Romans 11:6; Titus 2:11; Titus 3:7.)
2. Salvation is not achieved by works. (See Matthew 7:22, 23; Romans 3:20; Galatians 2:16; Ephesians 2:8, 9.)

IV. The Trinity.

Several of the "new religions" try to discredit the doctrine of the Trinity. Some accuse Christians of believing in multiple gods; others propose a different trinity, one other than the Christian view of the Father, Son, and Holy Ghost. Still others play semantic games with the term "Holy Ghost" or "Holy Spirit," claiming that it is a part of God the Father and that it really shouldn't be considered separately. The early Christian church spent literally centuries in working out the Christian position of the Trinity. The Bible speaks clearly to this Christian doctrine.

1. The nature of the Trinity. Jesus himself commanded, "Go ye therefore, and teach all nations, baptizing them in the name of the Father, and of the Son, and of the Holy Ghost" (Matthew 28:19). (Also, John 14:26; John 15:26; 2 Corinthians 13:14; 1 Peter 1:2.)

V. The Bible.

Many cults claim "new revelation" from God. The Christian faith believes the Bible is the complete revelation of God and that it is not to be added to or subtracted from. Just as Jesus, the Word in flesh, was the complete fulfillment of the Incarnation, the Bible, the written Word, is also complete.

1. The Bible is divinely inspired, not the work of men. (See Acts 1:16; 2 Timothy 3:16; 2 Peter 1:21.)
2. The Bible is not to be added to nor subtracted from. "And if any man shall take away from the words of the book of this

prophecy, God shall take away his part out of the book of life, and out of the holy city, and from the things which are written in this book" (Revelation 22:19). (Also, Deuteronomy 4:2.)

These are the distinctives of the Christian faith. Remember, though, Christianity is just that—faith. Ultimately, you cannot *prove* that you're right and someone else is wrong; you are a Christian because you have professed *faith* in Jesus Christ.

One interesting thing about these theological distinctives: they all point back to Christ. Indeed, all of Christianity revolves around Jesus Christ. So should you, in your witness to cult members, always point to the person of Jesus.

CONCLUDING THE CONVERSATION
There will come a time when you cannot or should not say any more. You'll have to sense this yourself. Sometimes the cult member, feeling cornered, will cease being cooperative. In such a case, you should wind things up congenially and leave. You won't be of any more help.

Most people make the mistake of pressing too hard. They don't know when to let go. They can't tell when they are saying too much. My advice is not to hope for a change, a conversion, right there on the spot. Rarely does God work that way. Besides, if the cult member feels as if you are trying to convert him or her, he or she will likely leave quickly. You may make the mistake of driving the cult member into a more resolute commitment to the cult.

Probably the most meaningful thing you can do for a cult member—an act that will speak volumes more than you could ever speak yourself—is a gesture of love and friendship. This might be something as simple as giving the person your coat, if it's cold, or buying him or her a meal, if he or she is hungry. (However, in no case should you give money.) It wouldn't hurt to give that person some information about yourself so that he or she can contact you personally in the future. (You may want to be discreet about this, say, by suggesting that he or she can reach you at your church.)

The point in communicating with a cult member is to show that person as much love as possible, to give him or her a glimpse of Christ in you. If cult members find love outside the cult, they have no reason to return to it.

Now if some of these things seem subtle to you—if they don't seem strong enough to combat the powers of the cult, remember that God does not always move like a raging flood. In my life some of the clearest messages from God have been as gentle (and subtle) as the dew falling.

A few winters ago in the Northeast a middle-aged woman walking across a parking lot spotted a girl selling flowers. The girl obviously belonged to some cult group. The girl was cold to the point of shivering as the woman approached. Without hesitation, the woman pulled off her cardigan sweater and put it around the girl's shoulders. The woman said, "I disagree with what you are doing, but I see that you are cold and I want you to have my sweater."

With that the woman walked away. The girl, stunned, later could not get the woman off her mind. Several days later the girl left the Unification Church. The girl stated that her reason for leaving was that she had finally found God's love when she found someone who loved her even while disagreeing with her. That, to me, is a powerful testimony of the power of God's love.

Don't be disappointed if you alone cannot change the mind of a cultist. Often it requires a combination of factors—maybe several loving, caring people—to come into a cultist's life before that person will change.

CASE STUDY: BARRY

Barry came from a good home. In fact, he was from the kind of home that might be considered ideal. He was a pastor's son.

The youngest child, Barry had been the favorite of his parents. He had been a faithful Christian and gave indication of a call to the ministry.

When Barry was a teenager, his parents moved from Pennsylvania to Alabama. Of course, it was a time of adjustment for the whole family, but it was especially difficult for Barry.

In time, he did adjust. Barry was able to make some close spiritual friends. But after graduation from high school Barry could never seem to settle down. He seemed restless, and it worried his parents. Growing inside him was a dissatisfaction with his spiritual life, and he longed for a more holy walk with God. Unfortunately, he found this difficult to express to the people around him.

One afternoon, a "Bible teacher" came to town, and Barry and his friends decided to go to hear the man speak. Within days, Barry and his friends joined the "Bible teacher" and his Divine Community Church.

Barry's parents were upset. But they trusted that soon their son would see the discrepancies within his newfound church. Weeks and months passed, but nothing happened.

The group was called the "Yellow Deli." They ran a chain of sandwich shops called the Yellow Deli and soon became quite prosperous. Their sphere of activity took in northeastern Alabama, northwestern Georgia, and southern Tennessee. The food they served was good, but the communities in those areas became concerned about the rise of cults so close to them.

In one small town in Alabama, eight young people joined the cult simultaneously. The small community was shocked. Some of the parents hired deprogrammers, with varying degrees of success. Barry's parents, meanwhile, continued to hold out.

Then, the Divine Community Church moved

to Vermont. Island Pond was the location, and soon scores of cult members began to arrive and settle in. Barry was one of them.

The people of Island Pond were outraged by this "invasion." To counter opposition, the Divine Community Church changed its name to Northeast Kingdom Church, and it began to establish businesses to serve the community.

By now Barry's parents were very worried. Barry had grown more distant and he had changed considerably. Since the group had moved to Vermont, of those from the "Alabama connection" only a few remained in the cult. Others had returned home. But Barry was one of those who remained.

Barry's father was convinced that if Barry could be talked with on a rational level, he might see the light and leave the cult. Ultimately Barry was persuaded to come home to Alabama for a visit. His father talked with him about the differences between what the cult proclaimed and what the Bible taught. Friends spoke with Barry over the phone. Barry was responsive, polite, and he asked many questions, but never did he give anyone the idea that he would leave the cult.

Then, as quickly as Barry had joined the cult, he left it. It probably was not so much what any one person had said or had done that made the difference, as it was the sum of *all* that had been said and done. It was a group effort that made Barry realize many people cared for him deeply.

As Christians we have the responsibility to

show others the love of Christ in us. How to deal with a Moonie? How to act in a sudden confrontation with a cult member? Display the love of Christ. It's that simple.

SEVEN

For parents of Moonies

One question put to me frequently is, "What can Christian parents do when their children join a cult?" It's a difficult question for me to answer, because the proper approach to such a problem depends upon the individual characteristics of the people involved. Each situation is different. Some young people need to be dealt with firmly. Others need time and freedom to make their own decisions.

Still there is some general counsel I can give on the subject, in the form of lists of Do's and Don'ts. These are suggestions that I can give you on the authority of my own experience as a Moonie and for the last seven years as an ex-Moonie who has worked with parents of cult members. Once again, these points should not be applied strictly—allowances should be made for individual differences.

Do's.
Contact someone who can give you specific advice concerning the cult that your child has

joined. For some of you, reading this book and learning about the Moonies has fulfilled the same function. Even so, having the advice and counsel of someone who has been through it —and having that person's help available whenever it is needed—is important. You'll find that questions pop up along the way. Also, an ex-cult member will help you understand the language of the cult. One warning: make sure the ex-cultist's faith in Jesus Christ is firmly established.

Feed the fire of faith. By consistently sharing your faith with your child in a cult you will encourage him to think about Jesus Christ. Perhaps you will feed doubts that have cropped up in his mind about his newfound religion. Positive reinforcement is the best encouragement for change.

Remember your children on special days. Never forget their birthdays, holidays, or special family days. Whether or not your child is doing what you want him to do, he is still your child. Nearly every cult calls itself "the family." If you leave your child out of your family, you have given him every reason to remain with his newfound "family." By sending him cards or letters or even gifts, you may remind him of pleasant times which may make him question his relationship to the cult.

Say "I love you" as often as possible. In many ways your love has been put on the line. Your child is being forced to choose between you and what he has been told is God's love.

Make your love the most unconditional. Tell him that no matter what he does you will always love him. God can work through that.

Pray! Claim the spiritual promises that God has given you. "Train up a child in the way he should go: and when he is old, he will not depart from it" (Proverbs 22:6). Your earnest pleas in behalf of your child will surely be heard by our loving heavenly Father. But be willing to wait on his timing, for he does have a purpose in it.

Share your burden with your Christian friends. Many, many parents are afraid of what their Christian friends might say if it were discovered that their child had joined a cult. But true Christian friends will not judge you; they will want to help you. Trying to bear the burden on your own can tire you to the point that you become less effective in dealing with your child. Other people can encourage you, pray for you and your child, watch for additional information, and even write or somehow communicate with your child.

Speak the truth to them in love. Share Scripture and spiritual truths with your children. Find those that would be particularly applicable to their new beliefs. Be careful not to become overbearing. One Scripture verse per conversation will be enough. Don't preach.

Realize that your child is now an adult. If you try to order him to leave, or in some other way treat him condescendingly, you've defeated your purpose. Your child will only want to stay

85

in the group to prove to you that he can make his own decisions. Don't require humiliation as a condition to come back home.

As well as the positive action that I have just outlined to you, there are also several things that you should *not* do.

Don'ts.
Don't overreact. Often a cult sets up parents to look Satanic by their reactions. "Only Satan would be shocked to find out that you are serving God with your total life. Thus, anyone who is shocked must be Satanic." Try to remain as calm as possible. In that way you convey a confidence that your God is in control.

Don't send in one of your other children to rescue your misled child. I know of too many cases where one child was sent to get another one out and both ended up in the cult. This very situation has happened to a well-known professor. Discovering that one of his sons had joined the Moonies, he sent another son in after him. Today, both sons have been in the Moonies for over eight years.

It's all right that your other children talk to your child in a cult, but make sure that it is always on your turf, not the cult's.

Don't try to lure your children out. Offering bribes or lures to return home only puts you in a weaker position. What you may think is divine inspiration can, to a confused child, look like Satan's temptation. Your child might look at "bribes" as being Satan-inspired.

Don't argue with your child. When you argue

with him, you only force him to defend the movement he has just joined. You can differ with your child without arguing with him. "Son, I don't agree with all that you are doing or believing, but I believe that the truth will win if you earnestly seek it out." In this way you do not put yourself at odds with your child. You are on his side. Let him know that you want him to find the truth for his own peace of mind, not for yours.

Don't compromise your Christian principles. One of the saddest cases I know is that of a woman who gave in to her child. She and her husband were divorced, and she so much feared losing her son to a cult that she pretended to approve of his actions. In the end she lost not only one child, but two to the cult. Her first son convinced her second son that "Mom thinks it's all right." Be firm, but be loving. Never compromise your principles. Your child will know that you have done this, and it will only serve to put you in a weaker position.

Never give up! Our God is a God of miracles. We often don't understand why these things happen to our families. But if we give up on our children, we have shortchanged God, too. For many parents, working through the cult problem has, in the long run, yielded great spiritual growth. Many parents have been saved after their children joined cults.

One family I know of in California sought for several months to get their child out of a cult. After many fruitless efforts, they began to realize that they offered their son no real alternative in coming home to them. They began to examine their lives and realized they were empty. In a matter of weeks they accepted Jesus Christ as their Lord and Savior and shared their son's predicament with their new Christian friends.

Their son, so impressed with the changes in his parents' lives, came home to find out what changed them. He received Jesus into his life and never again returned to the cult.

The point here is that God can make victories out of tragedies if we will only turn them over to him.

Deprogramming.

While I've already discussed this issue previously, it bears some special attention in regard to parental responsibility.

The problems with deprogramming are fourfold:

1. It often doesn't work.
2. As many as 50 percent of those deprogrammed return to the cult.
3. It can cause psychological and emotional damage that is worse than the cults' so-called "brainwashing."
4. Deprogramming assumes that a young person has been "programmed," or brainwashed—an assumption which hasn't been proven true.

But there are two other matters which I'd like to consider here: the legal ramifications of deprogramming and the Christian ethics of deprogramming.

First, deprogramming may be illegal, and attempts to regulate or eliminate the cults through legislation may be unwise.

I know of a case in which parents were sent to jail because they tried deprogramming. The child escaped during the deprogramming (and a lot do), and once back in the movement, pressed charges against her parents for kidnapping.

Many parents contend that cults cannot be considered religions. They argue that rights of free exercise should be withdrawn from cults. But who is to decide what is a church and what is not? The government? I'm afraid that once we grant the government power to determine the religious nature of groups, it won't be long before all churches come under governmental scrutiny and control.

In a free society the truth will win. It may not always win every battle, but it will win the war. If we make efforts to eliminate cults or other religious groups with which we disagree, have we not also abolished freedom? In a free society does one not also have the right to be wrong? I'm afraid we might be willing to sell our freedom in exchange for getting rid of religious cults.

Recently a state legislature considered a bill that would allow parents the right to hold their children if they thought the children had been unduly exposed to pressure. If the lives of children had changed drastically because of being exposed to that pressure, the bill provided the parents an avenue to legally step in and change it. Good idea?

What about the atheist parents' child who becomes Christian?

Wouldn't these parents then be allowed to take their child out of one of our churches? The same would be true of the Jewish parent who feels he's lost his child to a Christian church. Often what seems good in the short run can have drastic effects in the long run.

There is also a question as to whether it is wise for parents, by means of deprogramming, to take the situation into their own hands and out of the hands of God. Often, in the cases of deprogramming that I've seen, the decision to deprogram is born out of a lack of faith and patience.

Deprogramming leaves God out of the situation, it aborts the search for truth on the part of the cultist, and it is a method which effectively circumvents the spiritual work that God may be doing in the lives of parents as well.

God is all-powerful, all-knowing. He is aware and concerned about the cult situation in which your child is mired. He will work in his time.

God has no grandchildren. Our children do not inherit their relationship with God through us parents. They are children of God, just as we are. He works in their lives directly, not necessarily through the parents. We don't have the right to play God.

Before you make the decision to deprogram, you must ask yourselves several questions.

1. Is what I am doing legal? The Lord has always taught us to obey the laws of the land. A responsible Christian must consider this point.
2. Is deprogramming going to be effective? Often deprogramming does nothing more than emotionally break a child. Who is going to put your child back together after he is broken?
3. Can I afford it? You may think that I am cold-hearted to ask such a question. After all, who can place a dollar amount on the life of a human being? But taking into account that as many as 50 percent of those who are deprogrammed go back to their cult, is deprogramming worth it? Deprogrammers will offer no guarantee of success and will make you legally liable for all actions taken.
4. Are you doing this for your child's well-being or your own? This requires being honest with yourself. We parents cannot live our children's lives. The best we can do is offer them the benefit of our experiences.

Case study—Beth.

Early one Sunday morning my phone rang. When I answered it, I stepped into a crisis.

"Are you Chris Elkins, the . . . uh . . ."

"Ex-Moonie," I said, finishing the question.

"Yes," a woman's voice replied.

"I am," I said. There was a lot of tension in the voice. From the tone of her first words I sensed what she was getting ready to tell me.

"We want to talk with you about our daughter Beth," she said. I guessed that someone else was on the line with her. Her voice started to break. "Beth has just joined the Moonies," she said, "out in California."

"Are you sure it's the Moonies, not some other group?" I asked her. For many, the term "Moonies" becomes a catch-all for cults in general. "Is it the Unification Church?"

"Well, Beth calls it Creative Community Projects," a masculine voice—the other voice on the line—said. Beth's father continued, "We've heard that it's part of the Unification Church."

"You're quite right," I replied.

This wasn't the first time I had been consulted by parents of children who had entered cults. Often when this happens I feel as if I'm expected to be a miracle worker. Parents look to me for quick, sweeping solutions. But I find that each case is special and requires specific instruction and advice.

Beth's situation was a hopeful one. Her parents were contacting me within days after they had discovered their daughter's involvement. In fact, they had spoken to her only once before they had called me. And in their conversation with her, little was said.

It is often very difficult to undo a hasty

reaction or harsh words that are shared in the early conversations between parents and child. I thanked the Lord that we were not going to have to undo anything like that.

They proceeded to tell me about Beth. She was their only daughter and their youngest child. They spoke in glowing terms of her college career and how she had landed a prestigious job after graduation.

Theirs was a Christian home and she had been quite active in mission projects and youth work. Later, when I talked with the family's pastor, he stated how shocked he was that Beth was involved. "She was so sincere . . . and her heart was big."

I advised the parents to be as calm as possible in talking with Beth. She had been in the Moonies only a matter of days. She was still reachable. Her parents' action would probably be the determining action, one that would either bring Beth out or push her farther in.

Beth was only reacting to everything we had taught her in Sunday school. She had been led to believe that cultists were monsters and surely had red skin, horns, and pitch forks. When she met a group of clean-cut, disciplined, moral young people, the word "cult" never occurred to her.

We had also taught her that "God is love." When she saw all of the love that the Moonies had for her she figured that they had to be God's people. Perhaps we had failed her when she did not realize that God's love is *uncondi-*

tional love. Yes, the Moonies loved her, but only as long as she did everything she was told to do.

Beth's parents reacted wisely. They never questioned their daughter's wisdom or integrity. Instead, they voiced confidence and trust and told her that if she had really found God they would wholeheartedly support her. In fact, if she had the real thing, they wanted it too.

They encouraged her to come home and share with them her newfound truth. Since Beth had recently purchased a car, her parents used it as an instrument to bring her home. If she would come home and share her feelings directly with them, they would pick up the payments when she went back.

Beth later told me that her Unification Church friends were very negative about her going home. They accused her parents of having selfish motives and not really looking after her best interests. Yet, her parents were offering her unconditional love and trust. Beth was beginning to see where the real love in her life was coming from. Even when she went to board the plane, her Unification Church friends used threats to keep her from going.

All Beth needed was some scriptural evidence that the Unification Church was wrong. On a spiritual and emotional basis she had already felt it. She realized, too, that her parents had always been a great source of God's love in her life.

I spent one whole day talking with Beth. We went through the *Divine Principle* and I showed her where I felt it strayed from biblical teaching. Beth conducted a sincere search for the truth and carefully weighed the evidence. In the end, the truth won. Beth never went back.

Quite often you and I meet people much like Beth in parking lots and on our front doorsteps. Yet, many of us slam doors in their faces, we act as if we're not interested, and we're often rude.

I have to wonder what cultists think about our Lord after they meet one of us. Too often the cultist walks away thankful that he is not as cold and rude as we are.

If Beth had been depending on you to help her leave the Moonies, where would she be today?